SONGS SIGNS AND STORIES
by John Horton

Designed & Illustrated by Michael Kennedy

Teacher's Book One
ED 11409

Pupil's Edition 11409A

T0081262

Schott & Co. Ltd, London
48 Great Marlborough Street
London W1V 2BN

B. Schott's Söhne, Mainz

Schott Music Corporation, New York

FOREWORD

This series of music class books for the junior and middle school is the outcome of a belief that schools may welcome a progressive course for mixed ability music classes, planned on somewhat novel lines and ranging widely not only over the resources of music education but also beyond into other areas of the curriculum, while conserving much that has proved its value in our legacy of music-teaching from the past.

Thus side by side with experimentation in the properties of sound, the creative use of voices and instruments, the linking of music with other disciplines — language and literature, the visual arts, mathematics, natural science, history, geography — will be found a step-by-step introduction to the basic elements of musical perception and traditional notation, without which the most attractive schemes of integrated learning can fall apart for want of a clear sense of objectives.

At the same time one needs to be aware of the varied aims, organisational patterns, and social conditions to be found in junior and middle schools today. Where music is concerned, some teachers will handle the subject as specialists, others as general practitioners with musical interests. Some will prefer to keep music periods as self-contained units of the time-table, others will be anxious to make every possible connection with the rest of the curriculum. Some will place a high value on the aesthetic and emotional and intellectual challenges of music, others will regard singing, playing, and listening mainly as corporate and recreational activities. Some will wish to maintain the time-honoured class structure of the music lesson, while others will be intent on encouraging individual and group study. Some will make singing the centre, others will give priority to various forms of instrumental experience.

Since all these points of view have arguments to support them, it is not expected that every teacher, still less every pupil, will be content to dwell with the same amount of interest on each stage of the course as it is presented in the class books. A song or instrumental piece may prove attractive to one class, irrelevant to the ages or tastes of another. A topic or project may seem worth developing more elaborately through associated ideas and activities, and so cause a shift of emphasis or a departure from the printed sequence of material. Practising a particular musical skill of performance or

3

notation will receive more or less attention in the light of the pupils' previous experience or general abilities.

The following notes are offered by way of guidance in using the series as a whole. More specific suggestions are given under the heading *Teaching notes* at the end of each section of material.

Pupil's and teacher's books The teacher's books are so designed as to include all the material of the series of pupils' books, as indicated by marginal lines and page references. In addition the teacher is provided with supplementary information, suggestions for further research and activities, book lists, and harmonisations of most of the songs, with the melodies incorporated in the piano part on two staves.

The songs These, together with instrumental melodies, form the core of the musical material. Most of them are linked with the readings or stories, or with the various stages of musical perception and notation. They are drawn from many different cultures and periods, and many of them will probably be new to the classroom. Some are serious, some functional (work songs), some light-hearted and even frivolous. They also vary greatly in difficulty, and have been provided in sufficient numbers for a selection to be made according to the interests of teacher and children.

Readings and stories Introduced at intervals through the books, these are intended as backgrounds for songs, instrumental pieces, and musical expression of many kinds. They can also serve as points of departure for projects and integrated learning and discovery. While their vocabulary has been kept simple, it is hoped that they will do something to stimulate creative imagination. Both prose and verse passages are included.

Aural training and notation The elements of aural perception and of notation are presented, sometimes in unorthodox ways, step by step in close relationship with melodies, readings, projects, and individual activities. On no account should these parts of the course be regarded as doses of 'theory' — a misnomer that has done much disservice to music education in the past. Their purpose is in every sense *practical*. Essential symbols only are introduced, their function being shown as analogous to the many visual signs familiar to us all in everyday life. Certain firm principles have been followed: to present the symbol when, and only when, the sound impression it represents has been identified and isolated; to restrict the amount of notation employed to what is absolutely necessary for recording each stage of musical experience; and having introduced a sign, to use it from then onwards in a variety of contexts. Absolute pitch names — the musical letters of the alphabet or 'playing names'—are used side by side with the invaluable relative solfa or 'singing names'. French rhythm names, however, have been replaced by other devices for learning time values.

The pictures These are not merely decorative, though it is hoped that they will bring enjoyment for the eye to match the training of the musical ear. The full-page black-and-white plates have been carefully chosen both for their artistic merits and for their descriptive or imaginative details which can be related to the readings and suggestions for 'things to do'. The numerous diagrams and vignettes, specially designed for the series by Michael Kennedy, serve to illustrate the verbal text and set the atmosphere of the songs.

'Things to do' These throw out ideas for written or graphical work to be done mainly on an individual basis. Some require the writing of simple musical notation, a skill that is useful and not without enjoyment for at least a minority. Music writing helps to clarify and confirm details of musicianship, and can become an aesthetic experience in itself, like ordinary handwriting. If written notation is practised at this elementary level, however, it is best done in blank books or on loose blank sheets, with staves ruled as required, rather than in conventional music manuscript books, which are needlessly expensive for beginners and give little scope for setting out *short* passages in notation and interspersing them with drawings and answers to questions or other forms of literary expression.

The study of sound Sections dealing with the properties of sound are distributed over the pupils' books in the form of simple experiments, questions, and ideas for fuller exploration. Whenever possible these sections are connected with other reading matter and musical material. They are meant to arouse curiosity about the various ways in which sounds arise, and about their differences of pitch, duration, intensity, and quality.

Reference books The simpler and less expensive books suitable for young pupils to consult for themselves are starred *, and may be acquired for the school or class library. The unstarred titles are those of larger, more advanced, and more expensive books which are strongly recommended for the teacher's own reading and occasional use by pupils, especially for the illustrations they contain. These books can generally be obtained on loan through borough or county library services.

Instruments Among those that can be used in connection with the series may be mentioned:

(1) *Recorders* Some of the children will already be familiar with the descant recorder, and a few may have handled the larger sizes. The descant instrument is frequently referred to in the text, but to avoid overloading the pages with technical directions advice on playing has been avoided. It will be useful to keep recorder fingering charts ready for quick reference: there is a good set in Freda Dinn's book *The Recorder in School*, published by Schott & Co Ltd.

(2) *Strings* Any pupils learning the violin can be encouraged to demonstrate their instruments, and occasionally to attempt the easier melodies or add accompanying parts to them. The cello is a very useful item of music-room equipment, even if no one is learning it systematically, as it can provide the deeper sounds so often absent from

5

junior music-making. Its four open strings, gently plucked, quite often fit in with the essential primary tones of commonly-used keys like C, G, and D. The guitar, though generally thought of as a chord-playing instrument, can likewise supply single bass notes.

(3) *Piano* This is still without question the most helpful and versatile instrument for supporting voices and recorders, for providing a source of sounds distributed over its wide compass of seven octaves, and not least for its convenience as a means of visual reference. Even non-pianists can quickly learn their way round the black-and-white geography of the keyboard.

(4) *Percussion* This includes the pitch-percussion instruments, such as chime bars, glockenspiels, metallophones, and xylophones. These all make pleasant sounds, and can be played quietly by individual pupils in odd corners of the room without causing much disturbance to whatever else is going on. Like the piano keyboard they provide a visual map of the pitch-system, and their movable bars can be arranged and re-arranged in an almost infinite number of scales and chords. Good instruments are expensive, but economies may be made by investing in one or two diatonic sets and then adding extra notes (sharps and flats) as funds allow. It is not necessary to have more than one instrument of each kind, and quality is far more important than quantity. Unpitched percussion instruments are legion, and here the more types available the better, provided that they make a resonant, satisfying sound and are not mere toys.

ACKNOWLEDGEMENTS

The author would like to thank the following for permission to use material from their copyright publications:

E J Arnold & Son Ltd for *The Bee-swarm*, from *A European Folk Song Book* by John Horton

Boosey & Hawkes Music Publishers Ltd for *The Quern Tune*, words by A P Graves, from *The National Song Book*

Cassell & Collins Macmillan Publishers Ltd for an extract from *A Short History of Music* by Alfred Einstein

J B Cramer & Co Ltd for *The Carter's Health* and *Twankydillo*, from *English County Songs* edited by Lucy Broadwood

George Harrap & Co Ltd for *The Ballad of Semmerwater*, from *The Poems of Sir William Watson*, and for *Embustes*, from *Cancionero musical español* edited by E M Torne

Heinemann Educational Books Ltd for *Quand le meunier s'en va moudre* and *Quand j'étais chez mon père*, from *La France qui chante* edited by Bernard Fuller

Mr Gordon Hitchcock for *The Dilly Song*

Macmillan & Co Ltd for *Doshchiku*, from *Grove's Dictionary of Music* (5th edition)

Mr and Mrs Peter Opie and the Oxford University Press for the rhyme *A shoemaker makes shoes without leather*, from *The Oxford Dictionary of Nursery Rhymes*

The Oxford University Press for *Cocky Robin*, *Old Bald Eagle*, and *Philadelphia*, from *English Folk Songs from the Southern Appalachians* collected and edited by Cecil J Sharp, and for *Donkey Riding*, from *The Oxford Song Book* Vol. II edited by Thomas Wood

Penguin Books Ltd for *The New Navigation*, from *A Touch on the Times* edited by Roy Palmer

G Ricordi & Co for *Macaroni*, from *Eco di Napoli*

G Schirmer Publications Ltd for *Day dawns with freight to haul* and *The Moon*, from *The Botsford Collection of Folk Songs*, Vol. I

Stainer & Bell Ltd for *Grinding Song*, from *Twelve Manx Folk Songs*, Set 2

John Wilson for *Twenty, eighteen*, from *The New Fellowship Song Book* edited by Walford Davies

Uitgeverij De Toorts, Haarlem, for *Hebt je wel gehoord van de zevensprong*, from *Kinderzang en Kinderspel* and *Molenaartjes wind is zuidenwind*, from *Nederlands Volkslied*

Schofield & Sims Ltd for *Hark to the Mill-wheels*, from *Songs for Juniors* edited by John Horton

Schott & Co Ltd (London) for *Kemp's Jig*, from *English Lute Music* edited by David Lumsden (Ed Schott 10311)

B Schott's Söhne (Mainz) for *Siedzi sobie zając,* from *Das Lied der Völker* (1229), *Dívča, dívča*, and *Povedali, že som umrel* (Ibid, 1228), *Iz daleke zemlje husari ideju* (Ibid, 558), *O pescator dell' onde* (Ibid, 557)

Thanks are also due to those who have supplied pictorial illustrations, including: Mr E J Nicol and Lord Bridgeman for the photograph of the *Betley Window* (and to Mr Nicol for valuable information about it)

The Swiss National Tourist Office for the photograph of Weggis and Lake Lucerne

The National Gallery for the reproduction of *The Doges' Palace* by Francesco Guardi and Constable's *Salisbury Cathedral, with rainbow*

The Science Museum for the reproduction of an early engraving of German water-mills

The Victoria and Albert Museum for the photograph of the 15th-century wooden statue of Christ on a donkey

The Rothamsted Experimental Station for the reproduction of part of *The Woburn Sheep-Shearing* by George Garrard

The Mansell Collection for the reproduction of Baldini's engraving of *Theseus and Ariadne*

The Bibliothèque Municipale de Boulogne-sur-mer for the reproduction of *Crusaders attacking Saracens*

The Camera Press for Jane Bown's photograph of a field of barley

Grateful acknowledgements are made to the following, who have kindly answered enquiries or sent information:
Miss Jean Jenkins, The Horniman Museum and Library
Mr David Armitage, The Vaughan Williams Memorial Library
Mrs Jane Grigson
Mrs Nora Meninsky, The Arts Council of Great Britain
Mr N Gandy, The Museum, Keswick
Mrs Janet Bord
Miss Caroline Odgers, The Tate Gallery
Mr F M Underhill FSA, The Berkshire Archaeological Society
Miss Margaret Killip, The Manx Museum and National Trust

All piano arrangements are © John Horton unless otherwise stated.

CONTENTS (Book 1)

Subjects	Teacher's book	Pupil's book
Sounds as signals		
Pitch-patterns, letter-names GAB, solfa names, crotchet	17	3
More about signalling with sounds		
Major triad patterns, horn and trumpet calls, the 5-line stave, the note D	21	6
Clock chimes		
Westminster chimes, French bell tune, 'The little bell at Westminster', the minim sign, the note F sharp, the double bar	24	8
The G ladder		
Complete scale of G, tones and semitones, key-signature of one sharp, treble clef, 'We are the music makers', crotchet and minim rests, dotted minim, pulse, Moravian lullaby (2 - part)	29	13

Subjects	Teacher's book	Pupil's book
Patterns of beats		
Grouping of pulses in twos, threes, and fours, bar lines, up-beats, time-signatures, 'The busy farmer', 'Sheep-shearing day'	35	18
Longs and shorts		
Morse code, quavers in pairs and singly, 'There's a chicken on a wall', whole-bar rest,'Hot cross buns' (2-part canon), 'The wolf and the shepherd boy'	42	23
Changing the key-note		
D major, 'The hare that got away', 'Fire in the mountains', 'Black Monday', thirds (melodic and harmonic)	48	29
The wise fools of Gotham		
Story with creative work, 'The Gotham cuckoo' (round), 'In May we hear the cuckoo sing' (round)	57	37

10

Subjects	Teacher's book	Pupil's book
Some experiments with sounds **Vibrations and pitch**	64	43
Honey bees **'Sum, sum, sum', 'Bee round' (round),** **'The bee-swarm'**	69	47
A scale without sharps **C major, leger lines, solfa scale, 'Help me,** **Saint Nicholas', 'My lantern', hexachord,** **'Two rain spells', 'Shepherd's dance song'**	76	53
A useful time-pattern **Dotted crotchet with quaver, 'Turn again,** **Whittington' (round), 'Horse riding'** **(round), 'Bird of beauty', 'Wedding dance',** **'John Barleycorn'**	82	57

INDEX OF SONGS (Book 1)

Title or opening words	Source	Teacher's book	Pupil's book
Bee round	English	71	49
Bee-swarm, The	Latvian	72	50
Bells are ringing	French	25	9
Bird of beauty	Czech	85	60
Black Monday	Austrian	52	34
Busy farmer, The	German	36	19
Fire in the mountains	English	51	32
Gotham cuckoo, The	English	58	38
Hare that got away, The	Polish	49	30
Horse-riding	English round	84	59
Hot cross buns	English round	44	25
In May we hear the cuckoo sing	Dutch round	62	42

Title or opening words	Source	Teacher's book	Pupil's book
John Barleycorn	English	87	62
Little bell at Westminster, The	English round	26	10
My lantern	German	77	54
Rain spells, Two	Russian/English	78	55
Sheep-shearing day	English	39	22
Shepherd's dance song	Czech	79	56
Sum, sum, sum	German	69	47
There's a chicken on a wall	French	43	24
Turn again, Whittington	English round	83	58
We are the music makers	Moravian	30	14
Wedding dance	Slovak	86	61
Wolf and the shepherd boy, The	French	45	26

INDEX OF MELODIES WITHOUT WORDS (Book 1)

Title	Teacher's book	Pupil's book
Moravian Lullaby (two-part)	33	17
Westminster chimes	24	8
Hymn-tune from Freshford (Ireland)	90	65

14

LIST OF FULL PAGE ILLUSTRATIONS (Book 1)

	Teacher's book	Pupil's book
Sheep shearing and display of cattle from the painting *The Woburn Sheep-shearing* by George Garrard, now in Rothamsted Experimental Station	38	21
A field of barley photograph by Jane Bown	87	64

SOUNDS AS SIGNALS

Ambulances, fire engines, and police cars have a special signal to warn other traffic to give way to them. The signal has two different sounds, one higher than the other. The two sounds make a pattern like this:

These two sounds are usually just one step apart, and we can give them playing names which are letters of the alphabet, and also singing or solfa names:

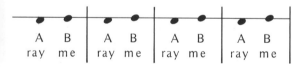

A	B	A	B	A	B	A	B
ray	me	ray	me	ray	me	ray	me

If you have a descant recorder you can easily play this pattern. Practise singing it too.

(Pupil's 3)

Suppose a vehicle needed a signal that was different from an ambulance, fire engine, or police car. It might have a three-note pattern that went up and down by steps.

To show the steps clearly we have had to use two lines, one for the G and the other for the B, and A fits into the space between them:

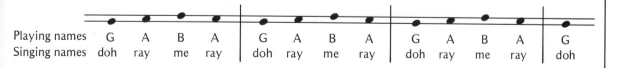

Playing names	G	A	B	A	G	A	B	A	G	A	B	A	G
Singing names	doh	ray	me	ray	doh	ray	me	ray	doh	ray	me	ray	doh

17

Play the three-note signal and sing it, and then find it on the piano. Here is a picture to help you.

[Notice the three black keys that stand close together, and then play a white key to the right of each black one.]

Playing names are the first seven letters of the alphabet: A B C D E F G. When they are all used up we start again.

Sound signals move up and down evenly and regularly. When we write out their patterns we can show that they are regular by fitting an upright stroke or 'stem' to each note:

G

(Our new 3-note signal)

A note with a black head and a stem attached to it is called a *crotchet*.

18

Things to do

1 Keep a diary of police car, fire engine, and ambulance signals that you hear, and try to write out their patterns. Notice that sometimes the signal begins with the top note of the pattern, and sometimes with the bottom one. Can you hear any difference between one vehicle and another?

2 Practise playing the 3 notes G A B on the recorder, the piano, and any other instruments you have.

3 Practise writing crotchets. Begin with the head, a neat oval shape, not too large:

Then fit on the upright stem, not too thick and not too long:

Sometimes the stem goes on the other way round:

4 If we have 3 different sounds, like GAB, there must be 1 x 2 x 3 ways of arranging them. (Work out that sum.) We have tried them in the order G A B and B A G. Find the other ways, play them and sing them, and then write them out, with a crotchet for each note. Of course you will need to draw two lines first (not too close, not too far apart).

5 Think of some more sounds that come in regular patterns. Here are a few:

> walking or running footsteps
> windscreen wipers
> dripping tap
> your own heart-beats

19

TEACHING NOTES

1 The G A signal is that of a fleet of ambulances stationed near the writer's home, and has been chosen as a convenient starting-point for pitch and time notation. The children will probably point out that the three kinds of vehicles mentioned do not all sound alike. It is worth taking this up in discussion, with attempts to make pitch-diagrams of different kinds.

2 Relative pitch names (solfa) are introduced as singing-names, with G as *doh,* The sequence G A B is of course one of the easiest to play on the descant recorder. These fixed pitch names (playing names) will need some extra discussion, especially if the children do not all understand alphabetical order.

3 The crotchet is given as the basic time symbol. A little practice in drawing it can be enjoyable as well as useful, as also can drawing two parallel lines for a rudimentary stave. The principle of alternate line and space for adjacent notes will need to be firmly established.

4 The mathematical idea of permutations can be introduced as suggested. (As the number of pitch-differences increases the results will be quite staggering!)

5 A book for the class library:

*Gordon A Perry *Fire and the Fire Service*
(Blandford Press)

MORE ABOUT SIGNALLING WITH SOUNDS

Long ago men out hunting or fighting in groups found ways of signalling to one another. They blew into the horns of dead animals, or hollow wooden tubes, or large shells. These made sounds that were louder than shouting, and could be heard over great distances. When working in metal had been discovered, they were able to use horns and trumpets modelled in copper or bronze or iron which gave an even louder and clearer set of signals.

Most of these instruments could only play a few different sounds, with jumps between them, something like this:

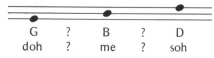

| G | ? | B | ? | D |
| doh | ? | me | ? | soh |

How can you tell by *looking* at these notes that there are jumps between the sounds? Which playing names have been jumped over, and which singing names?

(Pupil's 6)

But there was at least one more sound that could be made with instruments like horns and trumpets. This was another *soh*, a lower one, and if we want to write it we have to draw another line underneath the three we have already. While we are about it, we will draw yet another line at the top, making five altogether. We shall need all five lines very soon:

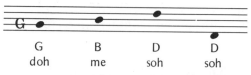

| G | B | D | D |
| doh | me | soh | soh |

Now we have two notes with the same playing name (D) and the same singing name (*soh*). The new D is an *octave* below the old one.

How many sounds do you have to jump over if you go straight from high D to low D?

Here are some horn or trumpet signals to play or sing:

TEACHING NOTES

1 The main purpose of this section is to build up a profile of the (major) scale through its principal sounds (*doh-me-soh*, with the lower *soh* also), and to show how these are written in the useful key of G.

2 To do this, we have slipped in without comment a new note (upper) D and given it its solfa name *soh* in this context. We have also introduced another line for (upper) D to stand on.

3 The fact that wind instruments like the bugle, trumpet, and horn are usually built in other keys than G has been avoided at the present stage in the interests of simplicity. It may, however, be raised by a pupil who happens to know something already about the instruments. It can be pointed out that in any case the pattern *doh-me-soh* occurs whatever the key may be.

4 The instruments as described here are of course the natural instruments as they existed before the invention of valves, with the facility for playing a complete scale that resulted. This development also can be ignored for the present unless it arises out of a pupil's special knowledge. A more likely question is how the players of the old signalling instruments made the different notes. The answer is that they learnt to tighten or slacken their lips on the small end of the tube when blowing. They were helped by the discovery that

22

picking out the notes by lip-tension was easier if one end of the tube was widened and shaped into a mouthpiece.

5 The limited selection of notes possible on the old instruments is due to the natural phenomenon known as the harmonic series. This is dealt with in an elementary way later in Book 3.

6 If the class seems ready for it, the notes *doh-me-soh* can be combined in group singing or playing as a triad or three-note chord. The use of hand-signs (fist, palm downwards, palm sideways) is a great help in teaching.

7 By the end of the section the normal 5-line stave has been brought into use, with a G placed (without comment) on the second line as a guiding beacon. Later this sign will be converted into the more usual ornate form of the treble clef.

8 Explain and teach the word *octave.*

9 The six little trumpet calls are for playing on recorders or other melodic instruments. It will help if the letter-names are found first. The calls can also be sung to solfa. Individual children can challenge the rest by picking out a call, playing it, and asking the other pupils to identify it by number.

CLOCK CHIMES

The Westminster chimes, which ring out every quarter of an hour from the clock tower of the Houses of Parliament, are played on four bells arranged to make a different pattern at each quarter, like this:

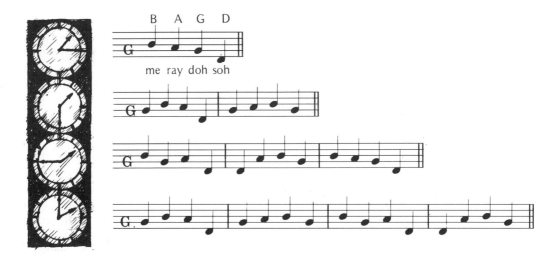

The pattern grows longer at each quarter until the full hour is reached, when we hear all sixteen notes (but still only four different bells). 'Big Ben' then follows with his deeper sound, which he strikes from one to twelve times.

We have given the letter-names or 'playing names' of the four notes that make up the first quarter, and underneath are the solfa or 'singing names'. Play these notes on any instruments you have, and sing them also. For the other quarters you must of course arrange the letter and solfa names in different orders, but remember there are still only four of each.

Another bell tune comes from France. It moves along most of the time in regular crotchets, but there are four places in the tune where you can see a note with an empty head. This is called a *minim*. When

24

we play or sing a note like this we must go on feeling the regular crotchet beats but make only one sound lasting for two beats. It will help to keep the minims the right length if someone quietly taps the beats on a drum, tambourine, or triangle:

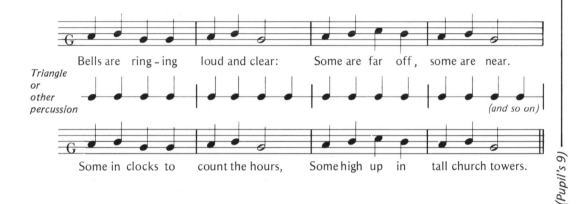

Bells are ring-ing loud and clear: Some are far off, some are near.

Triangle or other percussion

(and so on)

Some in clocks to count the hours, Some high up in tall church towers.

(Pupil's 9)

Our third bell tune is very short, but we can make it into a longer piece if we sing or play it as a *round.* To do this we divide our class or group in to three teams. Team 1 starts, and when it has played four notes Team 2 also starts from the beginning. Team 3 listens to Team 2, waits for it to play four notes, and then it is the time for Team 3 to start. Of course Teams 1 and 2 will get to the end first, but they can go straight back to the beginning and sing or play it all again. In fact it is quite a good idea for each of the three teams to play the whole tune three times over and then stop, each team dropping out in turn.

But before beginning at all we must learn

to find an extra note called F sharp. It is quite easy to find on the recorder, using two hands. On the piano it is one of the black keys:

If you are using a glockenspiel or xylophone you will have to take out the F bar and put in one marked F sharp or F♯. If you are using singing names, the name for the extra sound is *te.*

25

THE LITTLE BELL AT WESTMINSTER

[and so on, until each team has sung through the song three times, and then dropped out. Team 3 finishes alone.]

Things to do

Draw five parallel lines with narrow spaces between them. This is called a stave. Make a small capital G across the second line up to remind you of the name of this line and help to name the others more easily.

Now get ready to spell out some words on the stave. Each word has three letters. Make crotchets for the first and second letters, but a minim for the third letter. Then each word will have the same time pattern, but the heads of the crotchets or minims will stand on different lines or in different spaces. Here is an example: what word do these notes spell?

? ? ?

We have put two upright lines across the stave after the 'word'. This is called a *double bar*, and is like a full stop in writing words. Make a double bar after each word you spell in notes.

Now try these:

G A G   B E G
D A D   C A D
A G E   A C E
G A B   A D D

When you have written the notes, play or sing them. You can make this into a game with a partner, one playing and the other saying what the word is.

TEACHING NOTES

1 There is a great deal of new material in this section, which will probably have to be spread over several lessons.

2 The sound-patterns of the true Westminster chimes (on the quarters of the hour) are unlikely to be known by the children with any exactness. The chimes now fitted to many front doors are less elaborate, but worth bringing into the discussion as a familiar experience. The subject can also be linked with the various chime patterns of ice cream vans and the signal notes heard before announcements at stations and supermarkets. See article on *Chimes* in *The New Grove Dictionary of Music and Musicians*.

3 The new notation symbols introduced are
　　the *minim* (two-beat note)
　　the *sharp sign* (we *say* F sharp but *write and read* the sharp before the letter)
　　the *double bar* as a 'full stop' (ordinary bar-lines will be explained later).

4 Why bother with F sharp at such an early stage? Because we are still building up the profile of the extremely useful key of G, rather than starting with C major which has more complications than are usually suspected. F sharp is an easy note for recorders and strings, and is fun to locate on the piano keyboard.

5 The songs are very simple — almost nursery rhymes, but they fit in well at this stage. The round needs organisation, the chief points to observe being:

(a) make sure that everyone knows words and tune before attempting teamwork;
(b) see that the three teams are well balanced, with the abler children distributed evenly over them;
(c) quiet singing/playing is essential. Everyone should try to listen to everyone else, not ignore or drown them;
(d) keep absolute steadiness of beat, with no hurrying as the voices join in.

6 *Something to do* This may seem slender and trivial, but it is all much harder than it looks, and will need a lot of supervision and individual help. It should, however, provide some quiet relaxation after the excitement of working on the round. More than one set of lines may have to be drawn for the 'words'.

THE G LADDER

If we take all the notes we have used so far, and add an E on the bottom line of the stave, we can make two ladders, a long one and a short one:

The long ladder has five notes and starts from the singing name *doh* (playing name G). You can play all five notes on the recorder with left hand fingers only. All five are white keys on the piano.

The short ladder has only four notes, with G at the top and the black F sharp just below it.

The rungs or steps of these ladders all look the same distance apart, but some of them are really closer together than the others. These are the rungs with the singing names *me-fah* and *te-doh*. Whenever these pairs of singing names come together they make small steps, called *semitones*. The other steps are all alike and are called *whole tones*.

One of the semitones is the step between B and C. Find these two notes on the piano. Both are white keys. They have no black key between them. Why?

If we like we can make one long ladder, like this:

You can find these notes on the piano, but they are not quite so easy on the recorder, and you may not be able to reach the two highest with your voices.

Whenever *doh* is G we are sure to keep wanting F sharp instead of F. So to save time and trouble we hoist a sharp on to the top line of the stave, as a warning signal that *doh* is going to be G, and any note on the top line or in the bottom space is F sharp:

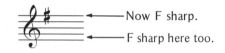

The G sign we have been putting on the second line of the stave is usually written and printed in an ornamental curly shape like this:

We will use this form of the G or *treble clef* in future.

WE ARE THE MUSIC MAKERS

Things to do

1 The song 'We are the music makers' comes from a part of Czechoslovakia called Moravia. Look for it on a map. The words mention several instruments. Try to find pictures of them.

2 Learn to write the new signs. A sharp is made of two small upright strokes with slanting strokes across them. When it is put on the stave, the line or space must show through the middle of the sign. Although we say 'F sharp', what we write is really 'sharp F'.

   The G or treble clef is a beautiful spiral, and we start making it on the second line of the stave and continue without lifting the pencil from the paper.

3 There are two more new signs in 'We are the music makers'. They mark silences or *rests*. When you see a crotchet rest like this 𝄽 or like this 𝄾 count one beat but do not sing or play any sound. The small black mark lying on a line of the stave is a minim rest, and tells you to keep silent while counting two beats:

4 Feel and count your pulse with the tips of your fingers against the other wrist, on the thumb side. Most young peoples' pulses beat about 80 times a minute, but the rate gets quicker when they run or are excited. Listen to a watch ticking. Is it quicker or slower than your pulse?

5 Here is another tune from Moravia to play on the recorder or other melodic instrument. It is a lullaby with only three different notes in it. Underneath is another tune, of four notes, which will fit the lullaby if both players count their beats at the same rate:

First player

Second player

[Remember—The bottom space is F sharp!]

The curved lines mean play smoothly, and only take breath at the end of a curve. The dot after the last minim for the second player means that this note is to be held for three beats. We call this a *dotted minim*. There is another one at the end of 'We are the music makers'.

TEACHING NOTES

1 'We are the music makers'. A more extended but easy song. Avoid dragging or making too strong an accent on the second word ('are'). There are opportunities for bringing in extra instruments, after discussing the words. The following could be possible:

recorder (= 'flute'), playing the melody throughout, or joining in for part of it.

violins similarly, the whole melody or parts of it, according to proficiency.

cello the bracketed notes (in the piano part) lie on open strings, and can be gently plucked and allowed to resonate through their written duration.

melodic percussion as for recorders and violins.

rhythmic percussion invent accompanying parts, especially for the dance section.

The crotchet and minim rests occur quite naturally and will cause no trouble in practice.

2 *Building the scale of G major* The approach is unorthodox, but relates more

33

closely to the structure of most melodies than does the rather artificial whole-octave *doh* to *doh* pattern, besides being aesthetically more attractive.

3 The difference between tones and semi-tones is pointed out, and the device of key signatures introduced, with the convention that the F sharp signature is 'hoisted', though the F sharp more likely to occur (in the lowest space) has no special indication. Note that the song 'We are the music makers' does not use the leading-note at all.

4 The usual form of the treble clef now appears.

5 The writing activities under *Things to do* may be omitted or reduced at discretion. Pulse-taking should arouse interest. If a ticking metronome is available its working can be demonstrated.

6 The two-part Moravian lullaby may be given to pairs or small groups of the abler pupils to work up on their own, after checking that the fingering of (low) F sharp has been mastered. Performance will be improved by attending to the phrase-markings, and a little slowing down in the last phrase will be found appropriate.

PATTERNS OF BEATS

When we feel a pulse, or listen to a clock or watch ticking, after a little while the beats seem to make a pattern, although they are really all alike. In our minds they make a pattern of *twos*:

1 2   1 2

or a pattern of *threes*:

1 2 3   1 2 3

or a pattern of *fours*:

1 2 3 4   1 2 3 4

These are the most usual patterns we seem to hear, but if we try we can imagine others.

In music these patterns are *not* imaginary. The first beat of a group of twos, threes, fours and so on actually is a little stronger than the others. We show the stronger beats when we write music by putting small upright strokes through the stave just before them. The strokes are called *bar-lines,* and the notes between one bar-line and the next make up a bar of music.

But the music does not always begin with a strong beat. Often the first note we hear or sing or play is on one of the weaker beats, so that the pattern is more like this:

2 1 2 1 2 1 2 1

3 1 2 3 1 2 3 1 2 3 1 2

4 1 2 3 4 1 2 3

If you look at the songs in this book, you can see that many of them start with one of these *up-beats*, as they are called.

Another thing we do to make the pattern clear is to put a special sign, or time-signature, on the stave right at the beginning of the music. There are several ways of doing this, but the sort of time-signature we will use for the present is $\frac{2}{4}$ to show there will be two beats in every bar

$\frac{3}{4}$ for patterns of three beats

$\frac{4}{4}$ for patterns of four beats.

(Pupil's 18)

35

Here are two songs to sing. One has a
pulse-pattern of threes, the other of fours.
One starts on an up-beat, the other on a
down-beat.

THE BUSY FARMER

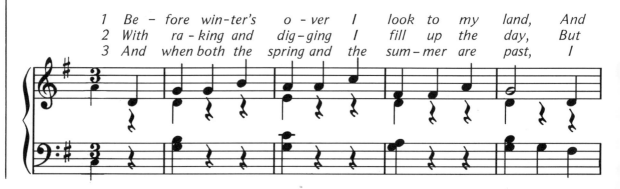

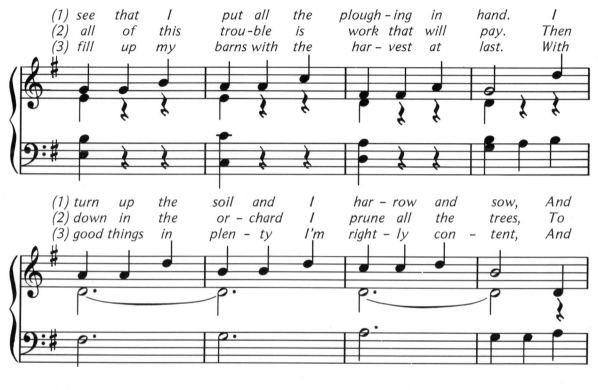

(1) see that I put all the plough-ing in hand. I
(2) all of this trou-ble is work that will pay. Then
(3) fill up my barns with the har-vest at last. With

(1) turn up the soil and I har-row and sow, And
(2) down in the or-chard I prune all the trees, To
(3) good things in plen-ty I'm right-ly con-tent, And

(1) bu-sy my-self with the crops that I grow.
(2) make them bear fruit with a taste that will please.
(3) say that the year has been ve-ry well spent.

(Pupil's 21)

SHEEP-SHEARING DAY

(Pupil's 22)

TEACHING NOTES

1 The way our minds tend to group regular pulses is a bit of practical psychology that may interest the children if there is plenty of experiment to demonstrate it. There are analogies with visual patterns which play an important part in modern mathematics teaching.

2 The grouping of musical pulses depends partly on accents, like those arising from walking, stamping, clapping and other bodily movements. There are also close links with words: two-beat rhythms in words like *Au-gust* (but the up-beat *Ju-ly*), three-beat words like *ter-rib-ly* (but the up-beat *re-mark-ab-ly*). Verses and jingles can be brought in also. The Edward Lear limericks, for example, are three-pulse with up-beat. One can also draw upon the wealth of street and playground rhymes; the invaluable collection by Iona and Peter Opie: *The Lore and Language of Schoolchildren* (Oxford Paperbacks) is strongly recommended.

3 The bar-line is introduced in this section, together with a simplified kind of time-signature. The conventional time-signatures may be learnt later, but they can be thoroughly confusing if treated (as they sometimes unfortunately are) as if they were fractions. It is best to accept the crotchet as the normal time unit, whatever old-fashioned theory books may say.

4 The two songs that follow are given in the pupils' books with melody and words. In both of them it is important to let the music move onwards naturally, avoiding heavy accents or too slow a speed.

LONGS AND SHORTS

In 1844 an American named Samuel Morse sent the first electric telegraph message between two towns. He invented a set of signals for all the letters of the alphabet, made up of long and short buzzes, or long and short flashes of light. These are called the *Morse Code*.

Here are some of the 'dashes' and 'dots' for a few letters of the Code:

D — •• (long and 2 shorts)

M — — (2 longs)

H •••• (4 shorts)

U •• — (2 shorts and a long)

Beside each letter you can see the longs and shorts written in musical notes. The long or 'dash' is like a crotchet or one-beat note. Two shorts or 'dots' are a pair of *quavers* or half-beats like this:

Sometimes we need to write one quaver on its own, with a small slanting tail fixed to its stem ♪, but when the quavers come as a pair they are usually fastened together by their tails.

Here is a little song from France, which you can sing either in English or French. There are only two different notes, A and G (*ray* and *doh*) until near the end, when the tune flies up to C and D (*fah* and *soh*):

42

THERE'S A CHICKEN ON A WALL

(Pupil's 24)

There's a chic–ken on a wall, Ea– ting all the crumbs that
U – ne pou– le sur un mur, Qui pi – co– tait du pain

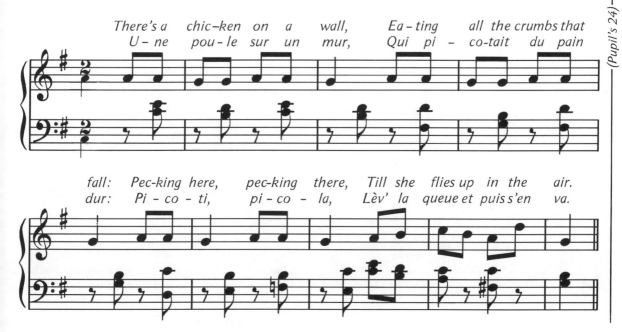

fall: Peck–ing here, peck–ing there, Till she flies up in the air.
dur: Pi – co – ti, pi – co – la, Lèv' la queue et puis s'en va.

43

Most people know the old street cry 'Hot cross buns', but you may not have tried it as a round. Here it is, with some help in singing or playing it. The 'leader' starts the song, and the 'follower' joins in with the same tune just one bar later. Of course the 'follower' finishes last. The small blocks hanging from the middle line of the stave are *whole-bar rests*. We have printed a few of the singing names. The key-signature of one sharp is not absolutely necessary for this tune — why not?

HOT CROSS BUNS

44

The sad song about the wolf and the sheep comes from France. Although it is quite long there are only five notes of the G ladder in the tune.

THE WOLF AND THE SHEPHERD BOY

1 My___ fa-ther's a far-mer, And I ten-ded his sheep. So I
2 There___ weren't ma-ny of them, And I watched them all day, But a
3 The___ wolf went on ea-ting, Un-til he was full, And___
4 I___carved out a flute from a___ bone that I found, And___

(Pupil's 26/27)

(1) went to the pas-ture, a good watch to keep. To
(2) wolf came and caught one and dragged it a - way. A -
(3) when he ran off he left on - ly the wool. The
(4) now my poor sheep makes a sor - row - ful sound. A

45

(1) keep, to keep, There weren't ma – ny of them, To
(2)-way, a – way, A wolf came and caught one, A –
(3) wool, the wool, And that's all he left me, The
(4) sound, a sound, My poor sheep is ma – king, A

(1) keep, to keep, A good watch to keep.
(2)-way, a – way, He dragged it a – way.
(3) wool, the wool, He left me the wool.
(4) sound, a sound, A sor – row – ful sound.

46

Things to do

1 Find out more about the Morse Code. Later on we shall borrow other signs from it to help with the musical ones. Just for the present try writing two more letters from the Morse Code as musical notes, using crotchets and pairs of quavers. These are:

X — ·· —

Z — — ··

2 Practise making quavers on paper.
For a single quaver begin with the head: ●

Then fit on the stem: ♩

Lastly put on the small slanting tail: ♪

Then try it the other way up: ♪

For a pair of quavers, make the two heads (not too close to each other): ● ●

Then add their stems: ♩ ♩

Lastly put on the tail joining the stems: ♫

Then try it the other way up: ♫

(Pupil's 28)

TEACHING NOTES

1 Quaver movement and symbols are introduced, chiefly in pairs as they often occur in this way in simple tunes. The connection with the Morse Code has been made, as it uses both sight and hearing, and depends in practice on the instantaneous recall of rhythmic concepts.

2 The first two songs are nursery rhymes, with a touch of sophistication in the first case through the possibility of using French words, and in the second by working the first section of the familiar street-cry as a two-part round. The terms 'leader' and 'follower' are suggested for their picturesqueness, besides having historical justification (*dux* and *comes* in the old counterpoint books).

3 The absence of leading note (F sharp) in these songs is worth noticing.

4 The whole-bar rest is introduced for the first time; it is better to stress this function rather than to relate it to the semibreve, which can lead to misunderstanding.

47

CHANGING THE KEY-NOTE

Up to now all our tunes have had G as *doh*. But any sound can be *doh*, and it is sometimes good to have a change. Suppose we decide that D is to be *doh*, and make a fresh ladder or scale. There will have to be an F sharp again, to make the semitone between *me* and *fah*. And then right at the top we shall have to use a new note, C sharp, to make the semitone between *te* and *doh*:

	D	E	F sharp	G	A	B	C sharp	D
	doh	*ray*	*me*	*fah*	*soh*	*lah*	*te*	*doh*

To save writing C sharp every time we want it, we put it into the key signature along with the F sharp we had before:

Whenever we see this two-sharp signature, we know that D is going to be *doh*.

C sharp is another of the black keys on the piano, and it has a special (and very easy) fingering on the recorder.

Here is a song written in the key of D. It comes from Poland, and tells of a hare that got the better of the hunters:

THE HARE THAT GOT AWAY

1 Once a lit-tle hare sat on the grass, on the grass,
2 Now the hare in ter - ror hears the horn, hears the horn,
3 There's no time for him to say good – day, say good – day,
4 Till he rea-ches safe - ty in the wood, in the wood,

(1) Thought he'd wait and let the hun – ters pass, hun-ters __ pass.
(2) Straight a – way he's up and in the corn, in the __ corn.
(3) And he does-n't have to ask the way, ask the __ way.
(4) Ly-ing in the grass now he feels good, he feels __ good.

(Pupil's 30)

49

(1) But the hun-ters soon were round him, Sure e-nough their dogs had found him:
(2) Pan-ting he runs through the clo-ver, But the dan-ger's still not o-ver:
(3) Though he's wear-y on he ru-shes, O-ver fur-rows, un-der bu-shes,
(4) In the mud the dogs are slip-ping, Head to foot the men are drip-ping,

(1) Run, hare, run! Run, hare, run!
(2) He's in view! He's in view!
(3) Like the wind! Like the wind!
(4) Home they go! Home they go!

'Fire in the mountains' is an old ring game. The inside circle sits or kneels on the floor. The outside circle, which must have one extra person, moves round. The inside circle sings, but stops suddenly at an agreed moment. The outside circle must try to find partners, and the player left over must then change places with someone from the inside circle.

FIRE IN THE MOUNTAINS

(Pupil's 33/34)

'Black Monday' used to be a favourite song for blacksmiths' apprentices to sing as they hammered away in the iron-working districts of Austria. As the midday meal was part of their wages they naturally took a great deal of interest in what there was for dinner.

BLACK MONDAY

1 On Mon-day, on Mon - day we have to earn our li - ving, And
2 On Tues-day, on Tues - day for some-thing good we're loo - king, And
3 On Wednesday, on Wednes-day there's no-thing else re - mai - ning, And
4 On Thurs-day, on Thurs - day the day for ear-ly clo - sing, And
5 On Fri - day, on Fri - day it's fish they will be fry - ing, And
6 On Saturday, on Sa-tur-day we're queu-ing for our mo - ney, And
7 On Sun - day, on Sun - day we can be la-ter ri - sing, For

(1) what was left from yes-ter-day for din-ner they'll be   gi – ving.
(2) while the mor-ning's work goes on we won-der what they're coo – king.
(3) if we've fin-ished all the meat the bones are not sus – tai – ning.
(4) when they've shut up all the shops the ow-ners will be   do – zing.
(5) if you don't like ea-ting fish then there's no harm in   try – ing.
(6) if we're not all paid in full then we don't find it   fun – ny.
(7) if we're fee-ling ra – ther tired it's real-ly not sur – pri – sing.

CHORUS That's all right,   we a – gree   life is for en - joy - ment, And

when the mo-ney's all been spent it's back to our em - ploy - ment.

Things to do

1 Find on maps the foreign countries some of our songs have come from. They include France, Germany, Austria, Czechoslovakia, and Poland.

2 Make sure of the D scale on any instruments you have. It is a very good scale for the descant recorder, because you can play all of its eight notes without 'overblowing'. On the piano you will need to use two black keys, and for tuned percussion you will need extra F sharp and C sharp bars or tubes. D is the best of all keys for the violin.

54

3 Set out the chime bars, glockenspiel, or
xylophone ready to play the D scale,
with an extra E at the top if possible.
Then take a beater in each hand and try a
kind of leapfrog exercise, like this (L
stands for left hand, R for right):

    L   R   L R   L R   L

If you add a *low* C sharp to the scale,
you can leapfrog downwards:

    R L   R L   R

These leapfrog jumps, missing out a step
of the scale every time, are called *thirds*.

Now use both beaters together so that
the thirds sound at the same time, making
a chain:

You can try all these exercises on the
piano, using the forefinger of each hand.

(Pupil's 35/36)

4 Make up some drum rhythms to go with 'Fire in the mountains'. Here are a few examples:

Invent others, and try changing from one pattern to another during the song. You can use other percussion instruments too, and make the piece longer by going through the tune several times.

5 Can you find other rhymes or songs like 'Black Monday', which mention all the days of the week?

TEACHING NOTES

1 The appearance of a fresh key will doubtless be a relief to all. It is immensely useful for classroom instruments, and time will be well spent in mastering the use of the extra sharp.

2 The three songs vary in length and difficulty, so that it may be best to select one or two only for learning. The idea of playing the traditional game of 'Fire in the mountain' is unlikely to appeal to any but the youngest juniors, but the song can be given more sophisticated treatment through the addition of percussion patterns, as suggested in *Things to do*. All possible combinations of crotchets, quaver pairs, and crotchet rests can be explored, and a percussion score built up, perhaps as a group activity by some of the abler children.

3 The exercises in broken and simultaneous thirds combine hand, eye and ear training, and lay a useful foundation for later study of interval and harmonic structure. These exercises again may be given to selected groups or individuals. It is not necessary, however, to restrict the piano keyboard experience to those who are having formal piano lessons: the forefinger 'chopsticks' technique can quickly be learnt by any normal pupil, and is a good way of developing a sense of keyboard geography.

THE WISE FOOLS OF GOTHAM

(Pupil's 37)

Gotham is a village a few miles away from the town of Nottingham. Long ago, in the reign of King John, the people of Gotham heard that the King was on his way to Nottingham and intended to pass through the village. They did not like this news at all, for someone had told them that any land the King walked or rode over at once became royal land. Their fields, their houses, their animals, and their crops would then belong to the King.

The people wondered how they could prevent King John from coming near their village. At last they agreed upon a plan. They would all pretend to be as stupid as possible, so that the King and his courtiers would not want to have anything to do with them.

Just as they expected, some of the King's men arrived one evening to tell them that he was near, and they were all to turn out in their best clothes to welcome him. One of the men blew a trumpet and another beat a drum to attract attention and make the

simple villagers believe that this was a very special occasion. But when the King's messengers reached the village they began to see strange things.

First, they saw a group of men and women hard at work making a kind of cage out of green branches, while the children were trying to catch a bird that fluttered around. Everyone was singing, but a few broke off their song to explain that they wanted to build a hedge round the cuckoo so that she could not fly away. Whenever the cuckoo left them it was always a sign that summer was over, so they thought that if they could somehow keep her in Gotham they might have lovely summer weather all the year round.

The King's men looked at each other, shook their heads, and went on a little further. Soon they saw a big round cheese rolling by, and then another and another. At the top of a small hill they found a group of people pushing yellow cheeses downhill as if they were cart wheels. When asked why they were doing this, they explained that they thought it was the quickest way to send the cheeses to be sold in Nottingham market.

The messengers again shook their heads. By this time it was getting dark and the moon had risen. In the middle of the village was a pond, and round it stood men and boys with fishing rods and nets. They were pointing to the middle of the pond, where the full moon was reflected in the water. "Look", they said "there is another moon, floating in the pond. If we can fish it out we shall have two moons instead of one, and our village will be better lit at night."

After hearing this, the messengers shrugged their shoulders and decided to give up. They agreed that the King could not possibly come to a village where all the people were mad, and they went back and advised their royal master to go to Nottingham by a different road. So the wise fools of Gotham had their own way after all.

MAKING MUSIC FOR THE STORY

1 *Music for the King's messengers* Make up a trumpet signal from these four notes:

You can play them in any order, and turn them into crotchets or quavers or a mixture of both. Use recorders, or melo-dicas if you have any — they sound quite trumpet-like. Make up some drum patterns too.

2 *The Gotham cuckoo round* This very old song is a round for three groups of singers. It also makes a good piece for recorders or other instruments. Group 1 starts the song, group 2 waits until group 1 has finished the first line of the music and then starts from the beginning, and group 3 starts last of all. Each group can sing the round through several times.

THE GOTHAM CUCKOO

(Pupil's 38)

3 *Rolling the cheeses* One way of making this into a sound-picture is to use drums of different sizes, with soft-headed sticks. The drum-strokes can suggest the rolling and bumping as the cheeses go down the hill. What will happen to the speed of the strokes as the rolling goes on? Will the sounds grow louder or softer as the cheeses continue their journey?

Another way of making the sound-picture is to invent a rolling tune that starts at the top of the scale and goes step by step down to the bottom. Here is an example, written in two lines so that it can be played like a round, using recorders or tuned percussion:

When 'leaders' and 'followers' are playing together they make a chain of *thirds*. The piece can be played through more than once. On arriving at the bottom of the scale the 'leaders' count two crotchet beats' silence, then three more (a whole-bar rest), and then start from the beginning again. The 'followers' play a D to finish their scale, count two beats' silence, then three more, and start again.

The real moon and the moon's reflection in the water

Here is a smooth tune for the real moon shining down from the sky:

And this is the same tune turned upside down, for the moon's reflection in the water:

(Pupil's 40)

When you can play both of them separately, try putting them together. This piece can be played several times over without stopping. Do not hurry, and be sure to count an exact 'one - two' for every minim.

The end of the story
Make up some more trumpet and drum music for the King's messengers as they leave the village, with the sounds dying away as they get further off.

Things to do

1 You can put the story and the music together, turning it either into a play or into a mime without spoken words.

2 You can make a set of pictures in the form of a strip cartoon or a wall-frieze to illustrate the story.

3 Here are some rhymes that have been written about the wise fools, imagining them setting out into the open sea. You could try illustrating these also, or perhaps even make up music for them:

(i)   Three wise men of Gotham
      went to sea in a bowl.
          If the bowl had been stronger,
          my tale had been longer.

60

(ii) In a bowl to sea went wise men three,
  On a brilliant night in June;
They carried a net, and their hearts were set
  On fishing up the moon.

The sea was calm, the air was balm,
  Not a breath stirred low or high,
And the moon, I trow, lay as bright below,
  And round as in the sky.

The wise men with the current went,
  Nor paddle nor oar had they,
And still as the grave they went on the wave,
  That they might not disturb their prey.

Far, far at sea were the wise men three,
  When their fishing-net they threw;
And at the throw, the moon below
  In a thousand fragments flew.

The sea was bright with dancing light
  Of a million million gleams,
Which the broken moon shot forth as soon
  As the net disturbed her beams.

They drew in their net: it was empty and wet,
  And they had lost their pain;
Soon ceased the play of each dancing ray,
  And the image was round again.

Three times they threw, three times they drew,
  And all the while were mute;
And evermore their wonder grew,
  Till they could not but dispute.

Their silence they broke, and each one spoke
  Full long, and loud, and clear;
A man at sea their voices three
  Full three leagues off might hear.

The three wise men got home again
   To their children and their wives;
But, touching their trip, and their net's vain dip,
   They disputed all their lives.

The wise men three could never agree
   Why they missed the promised boon.
They agreed alone that their net they had thrown,
   And they had not caught the moon.

(Pupil's 42)

4 This Dutch round is about the way the cuckoo changes her tune as the summer goes on. It is more difficult than the Gotham round because of the leaps in the tune, which start with a *third* and get gradually wider — a *fourth*, a *fifth*, a *sixth*, a *seventh*, and finally an *octave*:

IN MAY WE HEAR THE CUCKOO SING

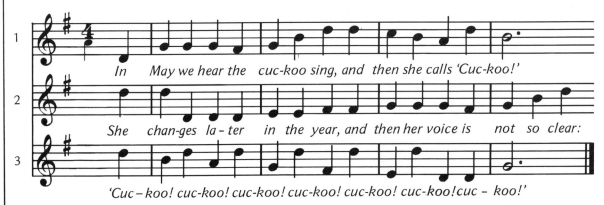

1. In May we hear the cuc-koo sing, and then she calls 'Cuc-koo!'

2. She chan-ges la - ter in the year, and then her voice is not so clear:

3. 'Cuc – koo! cuc-koo! cuc-koo! cuc-koo! cuc-koo! cuc-koo! cuc – koo!'

62

TEACHING NOTES

1 The story exists in several versions, not all
of them set in England. The inhabitants of
Mols, in Denmark, have a somewhat
similar reputation.

2 The traditional Gotham round is given
here in the conventional type of score.
The three voices follow one another at
three bars' distance, with the third voice
entering and finishing last. The whole
round can be sung through non-stop three
times over. It is suitable also for recorders
or violins.

3 The 'rolling cheese' and 'moon' music
offers further experience of part singing
or playing, with the use of chains of thirds
and the idea of inverting a melody. If the
hint to accelerate the 'rolling' theme is
adopted, it may be worth while to intro-
duce the Italian term *accelerando*.

4 The first rhyme is traditional. The longer
poem is by the Victorian author T. L.
Peacock. It is included here for older
pupils. Though apparently simple, it is
full of poetical imagery and symbolism.
Some of the images — such as the reflected moon breaking into fragments —
might give rise to imaginative sound
effects from glockenspiels and other percussion.

SOME EXPERIMENTS WITH SOUNDS

Experiment 1 Hold about 5 centimetres of an ordinary flat ruler firmly on a table near the edge, and use your other hand to twang the part of the ruler that is hanging over. You will see the ruler vibrate, and you will hear a sound: it may be just a buzz, or it may be something like a musical sound. This sound is caused by the vibrating wood pushing the air round it backwards and forwards and so making invisible waves in the air. Our ears catch the air-waves and send them to a part of the brain which recognises them as sounds — high or low, loud or soft.

Experiment 2 Throw a small stone into the middle of a pool or bowl of water and watch the ripples spread out. The stone has disturbed the water all round it, making a wave, and this in its turn starts a whole series of waves spreading from the centre of the pool or bowl to its edge. These water-waves can be seen, but air-waves are invisible.

Experiment 3 Hold one end of a skipping-rope and lay the rest straight out along the ground. Shake the end you are holding, and waves will travel along the rope. Each bit of the rope passes on its wave-movement to the next, but the rope stays where you laid it on the ground.

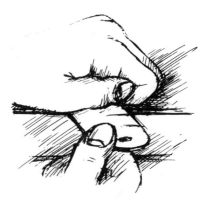

Experiment 4 Take the ruler again, and hold a slightly longer piece firmly on the table, so that there is less of it hanging over the edge. Twang it again. Do you notice any difference in the sound? Do you notice any change in the look of the vibrating wood? Try the same experiment several times, with different lengths of wood hanging over.

Experiment 5 Hold the finger-tips of one hand lightly against your throat, close to the 'Adam's apple', and hum (*m-m-m-m*) fairly loudly. What do you feel? Now do the same thing again, but this time keep your teeth apart and your lips lightly together. You will probably feel your lips vibrating, and perhaps other parts of your face too.

(Pupil's 44)

Experiment 6 Tie one end of a piece of fairly thin but smooth string, or a piece of thin wire, about one metre in length, to a hook in the wall or other firm support. Fasten to the other end a weight such as an ordinary brick, and hang the weight over a chair-back about the same height as the hook. Let the weight hang quite free so that it stretches the string tight. Twang the string to make a musical sound. Now move the chair a little nearer the wall, and twang again. What has happened to the sound?

Experiment 7 Keep the chair in the same position, but tie on more weight. This will make the string tighter, or as we say, increase the *tension*. What happens to the sound this time?

Experiment 8 Hold a strong elastic band stretched out in the air between your hands, or between two rulers. Ask someone to twang the elastic. Then try stretching the same elastic band over a small wooden box or drawer, and listen to it again. Which sound do you think is clearer and stronger? Can you explain the difference?

Experiment 9 Use a box similar to the one in Experiment 8, and stretch across it two elastic bands of the same length but different thickness. Compare their sounds.

What these experiments have shown

Copy these sentences and fill in each blank space with a suitable word:

1 A sound is caused when something ———— and makes waves in the ————.

2 Rapid vibrations make ———— sounds than slow ones.

3 The more a string is stretched, the ———— it sounds.

4 A thicker string makes a ———— sound than a thinner one, if both are the same length and have the same tension.

5 If a stretched string is twanged hard, it makes a ———— sound than if it is twanged gently, because the string moves further backwards and forwards. But the sound does not get ———— or ————.

6 A sound that is faint to begin with becomes ———— if we let it pass on its vibrations to a box or table.

(Pupil's 46)

TEACHING NOTES

1 Children are generally interested in the production and properties of sound, and enjoy experimenting with them.

2 Further sets of experiments, including the vibrations of wind instruments, will be given later. In the meantime, the teacher may like to apply the principles given in this section to any stringed instruments available.

3 A tuning fork is a most useful piece of equipment for demonstrating vibrations and the value of resonators (e.g. a table or desk top).

4 The written exercises are of a type that may not be favoured in every school, but they may prove helpful in settling the pupils down and consolidating the work after a busy practical session.

5 Books recommended:

Sounds, by Allan P. Sanday, with coloured pictures by Bernard H. Robinson. A Ladybird Leader Book.

Sound, by Henry Bruton, illustrated by Clifford Bayly. Published by Weidenfeld and Nicolson, 1963.

Sounds of Music, by Charles Taylor. BBC Publications, 1976.

HONEY BEES

To begin with, here is a very easy song about the bee.
(Remember to count through the crotchet rests.)

SUM, SUM, SUM

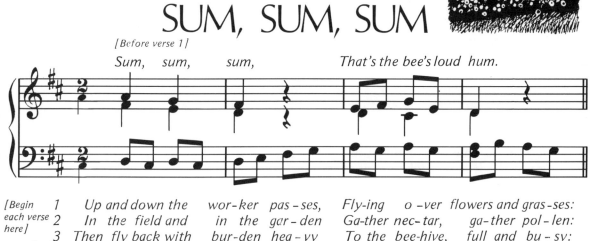

[Before verse 1]
Sum, sum, sum, That's the bee's loud hum.

[Begin each verse here]
1 Up and down the wor-ker pas-ses, Fly-ing o-ver flowers and gras-ses:
2 In the field and in the gar-den Ga-ther nec-tar, ga-ther pol-len:
3 Then fly back with bur-den hea-vy To the bee-hive, full and bu-sy:

(Pupil's 47)

[Sing this after each verse]
Sum, sum, sum, That's the bee's loud hum.

69

Of the many kinds of bees in the world, those most useful to man are the honey or hive bees. They live in colonies, usually in the hives or skeps placed ready for them by bee-keepers. Each colony has one queen bee, who is the largest and most important member of it and can lay two to three thousand eggs in a day. The rest of the colony is made up of several hundred drones or male bees, and many thousands of workers, which collect nectar and pollen from flowers, make honey and 'bee-bread' to feed the whole colony, make wax for the cells or combs, feed the grubs, chase out intruders, and keep the hive clean and cool. The worker bees even have a kind of dance to show one another where the best nectar can be found in gardens, fields and hedges.

From time to time one of the grubs that hatch out of the eggs is specially fed and looked after to become a queen bee. But there cannot be more than one queen reigning in a hive, and so either the old queen or the new one flies off, followed by a large number of workers and drones, to find another home. This is called swarming. If the bee-keeper sees that swarming is going on he attracts the homeless queen into an empty hive, where the rest of the swarm will follow her, make new wax cells, and start a fresh colony.

Queen bees and workers are armed with stings to defend the hive, but they do not usually attack human beings unless they are disturbed.

Country people used to believe that a swarm could be made to settle by banging metal pans and other noisy objects. There may be some truth in this. Bees have no sense of hearing, but they can probably feel vibrations in some way. A song that has come down to us from the days of the first Queen Elizabeth refers to this belief. It can be sung as a round, with as many as four groups joining in:

BEE ROUND

1 Bring out your ket - tle of

2 pur - est me - tal to

3 set - tle, to set - tle the

4 swarm of bees.

(Pupil's 49)

Another song about swarming bees comes from Latvia, on the Baltic Sea. It belongs to the days when every peasant liked to have a hive of bees in his garden, and if he found a swarm in the woods he could capture and keep it, on condition he paid a tax to the bee-ward, an official employed by the local land-owner.

THE BEE-SWARM

1 *Down the ri - ver floats a tree branch All with ho-ney - bees a-swar-ming,*
2 *Sad - ly there be - side the ri - ver Stands the bee-ward's bride a - wee-ping,*
3 *'If we lose you, bees so pre-cious, All our sum-mer joys will pe - rish,*
4 *'You with-out the wood-land flow-ers Could not ga-ther your sweet nec-tar,*

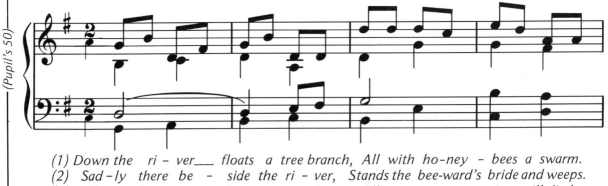

(1) *Down the ri - ver___ floats a tree branch, All with ho-ney - bees a swarm.*
(2) *Sad - ly there be - side the ri - ver, Stands the bee-ward's bride and weeps.*
(3) *If we lose you,___ bees so pre-cious, All our sum-mer___ joys will die.'*
(4) *So are we, dear___ bees, with-out you, Sad and drear the___ sum-mer through.'*

72

Things to do

1 Find out more about the lives of bees. One thing we have already learnt is that they cannot hear in the same way as man and animals do, nor have they any voices. They make their buzzing sound by moving their wings very rapidly as they fly or hover.

2 What shape are the wax cells in a beehive? Learn more about this shape, and where else it can be found in nature.

3 Collect sayings, rhymes, and stories about bees. In the Bible there is a strange story about Samson, the strong man, and his riddle that no one could solve. Part of the riddle was: 'Out of the strong came forth sweetness'. The story, with the answer, is in the Book of Judges, Chapter 14.

Here are some bee-rhymes to start your collection:

> 1) *Little bird of paradise,*
> *she works her work both neat and nice;*
> *she pleases God, she pleases man,*
> *she does the work that no man can.*

> 2) *If bees stay home, rain will soon come.*
> *If bees fly away, it will be a fine day.*

> 3) *A swarm of bees in May*
> *is worth a load of hay.*
> *A swarm of bees in June*
> *is worth a silver spoon.*
> *A swarm of bees in July*
> *is not worth a fly.*

4) How merrily looks the man that hath gold;
   he seemeth but twenty, though three score years old.
   How nimble the bee that flieth about
   and gathereth honey within and without.
   But men without money, and bees without honey,
   are nothing better than drones.

4 If you have piano lessons, you can find in a book called *The Show-booth for Bold Pianists* an interesting puzzle-piece by a Polish composer. It has the title 'An obstinate little bee', and can be put together in a different way each time you play it.

TEACHING NOTES

1 The topic is an endlessly fascinating one, and can be linked not only with music but also with environmental studies, biology, literature, the visual arts, and even with mathematics. From the many books available, the following can be recommended:

The Life of the Honey Bee, by Dr. W. Sinclair in the Ladybird Series, published by Ladybird Books Ltd., Loughborough. A small and simply written book, but up to date in its scientific information, and very attractively illustrated in colour.

The World of the Honey Bee, by Colin G. Butler. Revised edition, 1967 published by Collins. This is a book for older readers, with splendid coloured photographs.

2 The first song, 'Sum, sum, sum', may already be known in some version or other, and should be passed over if it seems too childish for a particular group. Its form, however, is not without interest, being a miniature rondo. The tune is a German folk melody, and the words are from the German of Hoffmann von Fallersleben, (1798-1874).

3 The round occurs in the medley *Country Cries* by Richard Dering (d. 1630). He adds to the four voices of the round an effective thrumming bass in crotchets on the note D (middle line of bass stave). This can be supplied by plucked or thrummed (*col legno*) cello, or on a bass xylophone.

4 The beautiful Latvian song is given in a slightly different melodic version, with another verse and a more elaborate piano accompaniment, in *A European Folk Song Book* by John Horton, published by E J Arnold & Son Ltd of Leeds.

5 The piano piece recommended is by Juliusz Łuciuk. *The Show-booth for Bold Pianists* is published in Edition Schott, 6575.

6 Other music inspired by the bee will suggest itself (the familiar Mendelssohn piece in the *Songs without Words*, however, was not so entitled by the composer, who probably had a spinning song in mind).

A SCALE WITHOUT SHARPS

So far we have used two scales, G and D. We chose them because they are easy to play on most instruments and comfortable to sing. We learnt that these two scales need sharps to make the semitones between *me* and *fah* and *te* and *doh*.

It is possible to make a scale that does not need any sharps. This is the scale that has C as *doh*. It is not very easy to play on the descant recorder, but it is the easiest of all scales to find and remember on the piano, as every step can be played with a white key — no black ones need be touched. And if you are using a xylophone or glockenspiel you will not have to change any of the wooden or metal bars.

Start on C on the piano and go steadily up to the next C, all on the white keys and not missing any out. On the way you will touch E and F; they make the *me — fah* semitone. At the top of the scale you will

play B and C, which give the *te — doh* semitone. These two pairs of keys have no black key between them, because they make sounds that are only a semitone apart. The piano is a scale-of-C instrument. All other scales on the keyboard need at least one black key to make them sound right.

Writing the scale of C has one problem we must solve before we go any further. If we start it from the top and go downwards we soon realise what the problem is:

C	B	A	G	F	E	D	C
doh	*te*	*lah*	*soh*	*fah*	*me*	*ray*	*doh*

We need one more note to finish the scale on bottom C (*doh*), but we have run out of lines on the stave. The only thing to do is to put in a small bit of extra line specially for this C. This is called a *leger line*:

C
doh

76

Hundreds of years ago, before singers had keyboard instruments like the piano to help them, the semitones used to give a lot of trouble, until an ingenious choirmaster named Guido (Guy) thought of fitting to the scale a set of syllables or 'singing names' very much like the 'solfa' we still use. Then the choir could practise going up and down the six-note ladder with the help of the 'singing names', making sure to sing a semitone between *me* and *fah*. When they had got this right, they would sometimes turn the ladder into a little prayer to St Nicholas, the patron saint of choristers:

doh   ray   me   fah   soh   lah,   lah   soh   fah   me   ray   doh.
Help me, Saint Ni - cho - las, help me to   sing   in tune.

Here is another song made out of the same six notes (or *hexachord*). It used to be sung in Germany by children who went round the streets after dark, carrying home-made lanterns:

MY LANTERN

lah   soh   me   soh   me doh
My   lan – tern, my   lan – tern,   Sun and moon and star - light, You can

shine up there, You can shine down here, But you don't have to put out my   lan-tern clear.

TWO RAIN SPELLS

The next song has only three different notes in it. It is an old magic song they used to sing in Russia, when the fields were dry and needed rain:

Come, rain, and fall down, and wa - ter all the fur-rows brown, Un -

- til the corn is fresh and green, and flies and gnats no more are seen.

There is a little English song which tries to do the opposite of the Russian one — it tells the rain to stop. We would have printed this one also without a key-signature, but decided to use G as *doh* instead. C would have made it awkward to sing. Can you think why?

Rain, rain, go to Spain and ne - ver-more come back a - gain.

For our last song, however, we go back to the C scale, but without using the leger-line C at all. The song is from Czecho-slovakia, and has a dance rhythm like a waltz:

SHEPHERD'S DANCE SONG

Sheep go wan-de-ring deep in the fo-rest, And all through the clea-rings they feed and they roam. I call them: 'Don't go in too far!' They an-swer: 'Baa,—baa,—baa!' Come back, sheep, for it's time we went home.

(Pupil's 56)

79

Things to do

1 Find out more about Saint Nicholas. He looked after choir singers, travellers, and children, and we also know him as Santa Claus.

2 The hexachord or scale of six notes can be arranged in 1 x 2 x 3 x 4 x 5 x 6 different ways. If you can work out this sum the answer will surprise you.

3 Practise writing C on a leger line below the five-line stave. Make the leger line short, thin, and the same distance below the stave as all the main lines are apart. Then put the head of a crotchet across the leger line, and add the stem pointing upwards. Practise writing D also. This note hangs from the bottom main line:

C   D

TEACHING NOTES

1 The 'open key' of C major is by no means as straightforward to sing, play or read and write as is sometimes thought, which is why we did *not* start with it.

2 Recorder fingerings are complicated and difficult to articulate in this key, particularly the lower ('middle') C and the F above it.

3 The 'white semitones' should be explored with eye and ear and fingers, using piano keyboard and tuned percussion.

4 The notation of middle C and the D next above it often cause some trouble, even to fairly advanced students.

5 The origin of the singing names, or solfa syllables attributed to Guido d'Arezzo can be found in greater detail in such works of reference as *The Oxford Companion to Music*. The information given under *Hexachord* may be helpful to the

teacher. At first *me-fah (mi-fa)* was the only pair of semitone names used in the system. Later the hexachord was supplanted by the complete octave scales, and the introduction of another pair, *te-doh*, became necessary.

6 The little solfa hexachord exercise, combined with a prayer to Saint Nicholas, is preserved (with Latin words) in a fifteenth century manuscript.

7 Some of the legends of Saint Nicholas form the subject of the well-known cantata by Benjamin Britten, parts of which might be played from one of the recordings available.

8 The songs 'My lantern', the old Russian 'Rain Spell', and the English 'Rain, rain, go to Spain' are all in the nature of primitive incantations, making use of a handful of notes representing the natural rise and fall of the voice. No piano settings are provided; they are best sung unaccompanied, or with improvised percussion.

9 The inclusion of yet another song about sheep calls for some excuse. The fact is that a large proportion of the best folk music has arisen in pastoral communities. This Czech example, with its waltz lilt, has a particular charm.

A USEFUL TIME-PATTERN

Work in pairs, or in two equal-size groups, A and B.
Both groups count aloud steadily: *one, two, one, two* and
then begin to clap.

Group A claps crotchets

Group B claps a crotchet and
two quavers

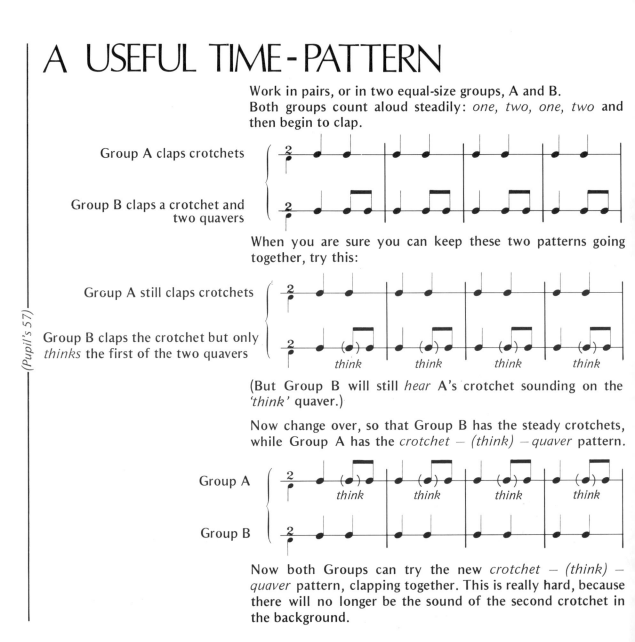

When you are sure you can keep these two patterns going
together, try this:

Group A still claps crotchets

Group B claps the crotchet but only
thinks the first of the two quavers

(But Group B will still *hear* A's crotchet sounding on the
'*think*' quaver.)

Now change over, so that Group B has the steady crotchets,
while Group A has the *crotchet – (think) – quaver* pattern.

Group A

Group B

Now both Groups can try the new *crotchet – (think) –
quaver* pattern, clapping together. This is really hard, because
there will no longer be the sound of the second crotchet in
the background.

There is a neat way of writing this new pattern. We write a crotchet, and after it a dot (to take the place of the missing quaver), and lastly the single quaver:

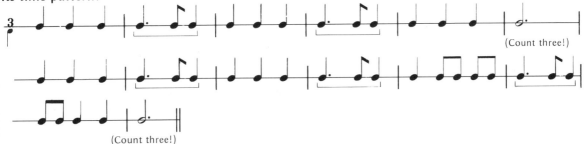

Now try this, and see if you can recognise a familiar tune from its time-pattern:

(Count three!)

(Count three!)

This time-pattern, *dotted crotchet — quaver*, occurs in hundreds of tunes. Here are a few to sing or play; the first two are rounds:

TURN AGAIN, WHITTINGTON

1   Turn a-gain Whittington,

2   thou worthy ci - ti-zen,

3   Lord Mayor of Lon-don.

HORSE-RIDING

1 *Horse to trot, to trot I say;*

2 *Am-ble and am-ble and make no stay;*

3 *Gal-lop and gal-lop and gal-lop a way.*

The next two songs have interesting shapes. We know already that the long curves or *slurs* over the notes remind us to try to sing or play each group of notes in one breath. They also show how many bars make up a phrase. In 'Bird of Beauty' the first phrase is four bars long, and so is the second. But what about the third and fourth phrases? In 'Wedding Dance' the first and second phrases are both three bars long. What about the third and fourth phrases?

BIRD OF BEAUTY

1 Bird of beau-ty, I a-dore__ you, All my
2 Bird of beau-ty, Can you doubt__ me? Do you

(1) life I've wai - ted for__ you; I have kept you
(2) think I'll live with-out__ you? Can you go a -

(1) al-ways in sight, Thought of you by day and by night.
(2) -way and leave me, As the ap-ple falls from the tree?

(Pupil's 60)

85

WEDDING DANCE

1 Look, they said, the old man's fi – nished, But you see I'm
2 We will have a jol – ly wed – ding When I've found a

(1) fit and spry. There's still time for me to mar – ry,
(2) lov – ing wife. There'll be mus – ic there'll be dan – cing,

(1) A – ny-way, I'm going to try.
(2) No-thing like en – joy – ing life.

(Pupil's 61)

A field of barley

JOHN BARLEYCORN

This fine old English country song tells the whole story of the sowing of seed, its growth, its harvesting, and its preparation for food and drink. The story of the seed is told as if it were a living person, who was buried, apparently died, came to life again, and then suffered more ill-treatment. All the processes, including ploughing, harrowing, sowing, harvesting, and threshing, were carried out by hand in the days when the song grew up. Now machines make the work easier, but the seed still has to be left to grow and ripen.

1 There came three men from—out the west Their vic-to-ry— to try, And—
2 They took a plough and ploughed him in, Laid clods u-pon— his head, And—
3 So there he lay for— three long weeks Till rain from heaven did fall; John—
4 There he re-mained till— mid-sum-mer And looked both pale and wan, For—
5 But soon men came with— their sharp scythes And chopped him off at knee; They—
6 And then they brought him— to a barn A prisoner to— en-dure; And—
7 Then they set men with— hol-ly clubs To beat him flesh— from bones; The—
8 O Bar-ley-corn's the— choi-cest grain That e'er was sown— on land. It—

(1) they have made a   so-lemn oath John__ Bar-ley-corn should die: _____
(2) then they made a   so-lemn oath John__ Bar-ley-corn was   dead:_____
(3) Bar-ley-corn sprang up a-gain And__ that sur-prised them all: _____
(4) all he had a   spi-ky beard To__ show he was a   man: _____
(5) rolled and tied him by the waist And__ served him bar-b'rous-ly: _____
(6) then they fetched him out a-gain And__ laid him on the floor: _____
(7) mil-ler served him worse than that, He__ ground him 'tween two stones: _____
(8) will do more than a-ny grain By__ tur-ning of your hand: _____

Sing

ri-fol-lol, the did-dle all the day, Ri-fol-le-ro dee.

(Pupil's 63)

Things to do

1 Practise writing the dotted crotchet — quaver pattern:

♩. ♪   Keep the dot

small and not too far away from the crotchet-head.

2 Make up a mime to the story of John Barleycorn, or a set of pictures to illustrate it.

3 Here is an old Irish hymn-tune that has lost its words. Play it on recorders or other instruments, and then see if you can make up some words to fit. The line marked 'accompaniment' is for another instrument to act as partner.

HYMN-TUNE FROM FRESHFORD (IRELAND)

TEACHING NOTES

1 The time-pattern ♩. ♪ occurs so frequently that it is worthwhile mastering it at this stage through pulse, sound, and symbols. The suggested approach will, it is hoped, lead to greater security and

understanding than a mere arithmetical knowledge of the formula.

2 The Whittington round will almost certainly be known to some pupils, but it provides additional ear and eye practice in the new time-pattern. 'Horse Riding' will be less familiar. A suitable tempo is essential. Rhythmic accompaniment for untuned percussion might be devised.

3 'Bird of Beauty' is Czech, 'Wedding Dance' is Slovakian. The charm of both melodies is due to their unusual phrase-structure, as pointed out in the text.

4 'John Barleycorn' is one of the greatest of all English folk-ballads, and exists in many different versions of tune and words. It holds a wealth of possibilities for related studies and projects. The imagery — almost certainly pre-Christian — of suffering, death, burial, and resurrection led Bernard Shaw to declare (in the preface to his play *Androcles and the Lion*) that 'John Barleycorn' might be a starting-point for a liberal scheme of religious education. The use of mime and dance would also be worth exploring.

5 An inexpensive book, giving up-to-date information on grain crops and many other country matters, is *Farming*, by Peter Rice. It is clearly and attractively illustrated in colour by the author, and is published for the National Trust by Dinosaur Publications Ltd, Over, Cambridge.

6 Mathematically-minded pupils might be interested to know that in pre-decimal times the 'barleycorn' was a measure of length equivalent to a third of an inch. A useless but amusing marathon Victorian sum asked: 'Assuming that the circumference of the earth at the Equator is 24,902 miles, how many barleycorns would reach round the earth?'

7 The hymn tune or chant from Freshford in Ireland is taken from the Petrie collection of Irish traditional music. It is given here to provide additional work (part-playing and word composition) for the quicker pupils, perhaps working in pairs, although the two-part setting is playable by one person on tuned percussion (two beaters) or piano.